ANIMALS OF THE CHINESE ZODIAC

MEET YOUR MATCH!

AN ILLUSTRATED GUIDE TO THE 12 SIGNS

written by
TERESA ROBESON

illustrated by
PING ZHU

CONTENTS

ANIMALS OF THE CHINESE ZODIAC

MEET YOUR MATCH!

AN ILLUSTRATED GUIDE TO THE 12 SIGNS

written by
TERESA ROBESON

illustrated by
PING ZHU

CONTENTS

ENTER THE

CHINESE ZODIAC

新年快乐

HAPPY NEW YEAR!

XIN NIAN KUAI LE

Laughter and music bloom on the streets. Firecrackers pop and drums boom. Lively lion and colorful dragon parades dance by. Everyone is celebrating the start of a new year!

In many parts of the world, the New Year is a holiday for only one day on January 1. But in China and lots of the Asian countries, the New Year can be anytime in the months of January and February. That's because a lunar calendar doesn't match up to the one we know that starts in January and ends in December.

The New Year is not just a number... it's also an animal! Each year is paired with one of twelve incredible animals. For example, 2026 was the Year of the Horse. Some people believe that the animal of the year you're born in can help tell you about your personality. This tradition is known as the Chinese zodiac.

THE ANIMALS WERE EXCITED. WHO WOULDN'T WANT TO BE HONORED IN SUCH A WAY?

The morning of the race dawned. Animals scampered, scurried, stomped, and slithered toward the Jade Palace.

1 Rat stared at the roaring river. She would never be able to cross it on her own. But she knew who could: Ox. Built like a sturdy house, Ox would not be swept away. He was also a kind soul who liked to help others.

Rat said in her sweetest voice, "Dear Ox, I'm too tiny to swim across the river. Would you let me sit on your back? I'm so light that you wouldn't notice me at all."

As she expected, Ox said yes.

2 Strong Ox plowed through the churning river like a torpedo. Even muscular Tiger, who jumped in at the same time, could not keep up.

3 When the shore was just a whisker away, Rat took a giant leap off Ox's back, landing right at the feet of the Jade Emperor.

"First place, little Rat." The Emperor beamed. "Well done."

"Harumph," said Ox, who stomped onto shore after Rat. But he didn't hold a grudge for long. And he could live with second place.

4 Then Tiger sprung out of the river with a roar. He shook himself, spraying water everywhere. Water dripped off the Emperor's beard as he looked down at his wet robes in dismay. He frowned at Tiger but gave him third place.

5 Rabbit, swift and nimble, arrived next. She had hopped over on stones that jutted out of the river.

HOW DOES IT WORK?

There are twelve animals in the Chinese zodiac. They appear in a cycle that repeats every twelve years. These animals are called zodiac signs.

Your zodiac sign is said to predict things about your personality, such as whether you are into sports or like to hang out with a crowd. It also suggests who you might get along with and what jobs you might enjoy. But the zodiac is not only about animals. Each year is also linked to five elements of nature: Wood, Fire, Earth, Metal, and Water. Like adding seasoning to food, your element mixes with your animal sign to make the unique "flavor" of your personality!

WOOD

FIRE

EARTH

METAL

WATER

HOW DOES IT HELP US?

If the world sometimes seems mysterious to you, imagine how people a few thousand years ago must have felt. They didn't have the science or technology to understand why things happen. The zodiac helped life feel less confusing. That's probably why it became an important part of Chinese people's lives.

These days, people around the world also use it as a fun way to describe themselves or get to know someone. This book will be your guide to joining in the fun!

First, let's look at how the Chinese zodiac came to be over two thousand years ago. Stories vary, but legend has it that the animal signs were chosen by competing in a race....

THE GREAT RACE

LONG, LONG AGO, NO ONE KEPT TRACK OF THE YEARS. THE JADE EMPEROR, RULER OF HEAVEN AND EARTH, DECIDED SOMETHING NEEDED TO BE DONE ABOUT THIS.

"There shall be a cycle of twelve years," he proclaimed. "All the creatures in my kingdom are invited to a great race. The first twelve to cross the river and arrive on the shores of my palace will have a year named after them."

9 Eighth, ninth, and tenth places were taken by Goat, Monkey, and Rooster. They arrived as a group, having joined forces to build a raft. Paddling together, they were able to arrive in time.

10 Soaking wet, Dog popped out of the water, carrying a stick. After dropping the stick proudly at the Emperor's feet, Dog prepared to shake himself dry.

"NO!" everyone yelled.

The Emperor held up a hand to shield his face. "You are in eleventh place. Now run far from us before you shake."

11 Snort! Covered in dirt, Pig plodded toward the group.

"Were you already on the shore this whole time?" The Emperor shook his head in disbelief.

Pig scratched some dirt out of his ear. "I found a mud hole by the water's edge and couldn't resist."

Jade Emperor chuckled. "Well, Pig, you are just in time to be the final animal in my new calendar." He clapped his hands together. "Now let us celebrate with a feast in my palace."

"Good," grunted Pig. "I'm starving!"

MEET YOUR MATCH!

YOUR BIRTH ANIMAL

LOOK FOR YOUR BIRTH YEAR ON THESE PAGES TO DISCOVER YOUR ANIMAL SIGN!

TURN TO THE PAGE NUMBER UNDER YOUR ZODIAC ANIMAL TO FIND OUT MORE.

鼠	牛	虎	兔	龍	蛇
RAT	OX	TIGER	RABBIT	DRAGON	SNAKE
TURN TO P16	TURN TO P20	TURN TO P24	TURN TO P28	TURN TO P32	TURN TO P36
1924	1925	1926	1927	1928	1929
1936	1937	1938	1939	1940	1941
1948	1949	1950	1951	1952	1953
1960	1961	1962	1963	1964	1965
1972	1973	1974	1975	1976	1977
1984	1985	1986	1987	1988	1989
1996	1997	1998	1999	2000	2001
2008	2009	2010	2011	2012	2013
2020	2021	2022	2023	2024	2025
2032	2033	2034	2035	2036	2037
2044	2045	2046	2047	2048	2049

6 Suddenly, a shadow fell over the group. Dragon blocked the sun briefly as he swooped down to the shore and took the fifth spot.

"I thought you would be first," said the Jade Emperor.

Dragon bowed respectfully. "I flew over a village where everything was dried up. I brought them some much needed rain before continuing."

The Emperor smiled, pleased at Dragon's good deed.

7 Just then Horse splashed out from the water, tossing her mane. She didn't know Snake had clung to her back leg in the river. Now he let go and launched himself into sixth place.

Horse took seventh, grumbling about Snake under her breath.

8 "Is anyone else coming?" growled Tiger impatiently.

馬 HORSE	羊 GOAT	猴 MONKEY	雞 ROOSTER	狗 DOG	豬 PIG
TURN TO P40	TURN TO P44	TURN TO P48	TURN TO P52	TURN TO P56	TURN TO P60
1930	1931	1932	1933	1934	1935
1942	1943	1944	1945	1946	1947
1954	1955	1956	1957	1958	1959
1966	1967	1968	1969	1970	1971
1978	1979	1980	1981	1982	1983
1990	1991	1992	1993	1994	1995
2002	2003	2004	2005	2006	2007
2014	2015	2016	2017	2018	2019
2026	2027	2028	2029	2030	2031
2038	2039	2040	2041	2042	2043
2050	2051	2052	2053	2054	2055

NOW MIX IN YOUR ELEMENT!

Remember, your year is not just about the animal but also an added element. This means that a Wood Pig is different from a Fire Pig, even though they are both born in a Year of the Pig. Look up your birth year to see what your element is.

* **WOOD:** Years ending in 4 or 5. Wood people are good listeners, as well as kind and loyal.
* **FIRE:** Years ending in 6 or 7. Fire people have a natural glow. They sometimes speak too quickly.
* **EARTH:** Years ending in 8 or 9. Earth people are calm and easy to get along with.
* **METAL:** Years ending in 0 or 1. Metal people have good manners and are full of courage.
* **WATER:** Years ending in 2 or 3. Water people are flexible, gentle, and go with the flow.

Want to know more about element-animal pairings? Look out for the "Element-ary" boxes throughout this book.

NOT SURE YOUR BIRTH ANIMAL FITS YOU?

No problem! Turn the page to meet another match!

PLAY THE GAME TO

FIND ANOTHER MATCH!

Do you sometimes feel not quite yourself? It can be that way with your Chinese zodiac sign, too. Maybe you feel like a different animal. Play this game to see what that alternate sign might be!

Start by answering the question on the left of the chart. Follow the path of your answers to find an animal that might fit you better. Then turn to the page number next to that animal and see if you've found a better match.

You can play this game over and over. Depending on your choices, you could be a completely different animal each time!

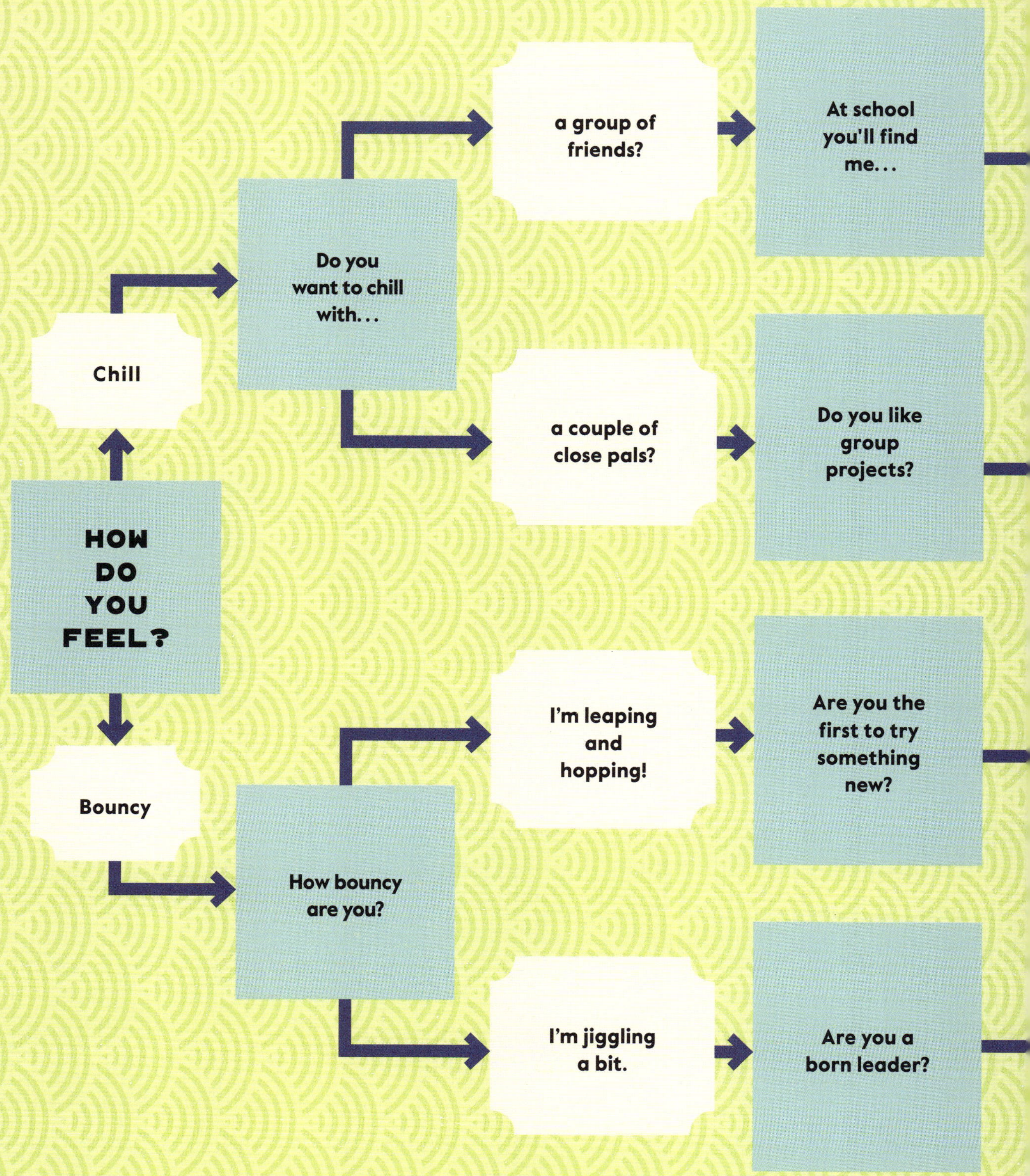

feeling myself in a new pair of shoes.

SNAKE
TURN TO P36

helping my friends with their homework.

DOG
TURN TO P56

Yes, I do!

At the park, I like to...

enjoy a nature walk.

GOAT
TURN TO P44

read a book under a tree.

ROOSTER
TURN TO P52

Not so much.

I like to spend time...

expressing myself through music.

RABBIT
TURN TO P28

working on a project on my own.

OX
TURN TO P20

Yes, I love new adventures!

TIGER
TURN TO P24

Not always...

Everyone knows me because...

I'm the captain of my sports team.

HORSE
TURN TO P40

I'm the class clown.

MONKEY
TURN TO P48

I'm more of a team player.

At a party you'll find me...

chatting with everyone in the room.

RAT
TURN TO P16

sharing a batch of sweet cupcakes.

PIG
TURN TO P60

I rule the castle!

DRAGON
TURN TO P32

鼠

SHU

THE RAT

1924 1936 1948 1960 1972

1984 1996 2008 2020 2032 2044

YOU ARE THE

RAT

HOORAY! BEING QUICK OF MIND AND FEET, YOU BECAME THE FIRST ZODIAC SIGN.

Real rats may be small, but people born in the Rat year often have big personalities. You're probably chatty and friendly, so you might get invited to a lot of parties. That's lucky because Rats normally like to hang out with others rather than spend time alone.

Like the Rat convincing Ox to help her, you may also be clever, creative, and charming. But you can get annoyed quickly, so be careful not to snap at your friends. Let your friendliness smooth over fights.

THE NAME'S THE SAME

Even though we call it the Year of the Rat, the Chinese word 鼠 can mean either mouse or rat. Are you quiet like a mouse or as bold as a rat?

JUST FOR FUN

Reading could be one of your favorite hobbies.

While you often have your nose—and whiskers—in a book, you also love to play with friends. You could like cooking too because rats enjoy food!

FINDING FRIENDS

Your best friend might be Ox—they have the patience to put up with your scrambling around. Dragons also make good buddies for Rats. They are as likeable as you, and you could be a popular pair.

GREAT JOBS

You have so many talents.

You could be a super salesperson with your charm, a terrific writer with your creativity, or a keen detective with your cleverness.

DO YOU DROOL OVER CHIPS?

If so, you can blame it on being a Rat. Your favorite flavor is salty.

ELEMENT-ARY

If you were born in 2020, you're a Metal Rat.

Not only do you have all the usual Rat qualities, but you might also be brave and organized.

FEELING LUCKY?

LUCKY NUMBERS

2 3

LUCKY COLOR

BLUE

LUCKY FLOWER

LILY

DON'T FEEL LIKE A RAT?

You are one smart cookie. But what if you're also extra brave? Go to page 32!

Or go to page 14 to replay the game.

牛

NIU

THE OX

1925 **1937** **1949** **1961** **1973**

1985 1997 2009 2021 2033 2045

YOU ARE THE

OX

OX SHOWS THE WORLD THAT SLOW AND STEADY CAN ALMOST WIN THE RACE...

... if only Rat hadn't hitched a ride to finish first.

As an Ox, getting a big project done can make you feel great. It's so satisfying to paint that birdhouse or put up holiday decorations by yourself.

Not one for crowds, you might enjoy being alone or hanging out with a small group of close friends. They know they can depend on you because you're usually generous. You don't ask for praise (but you don't mind getting it!).

You are honest and patient, but sometimes you can be too serious. To make yourself laugh, you could read a joke book or watch a funny movie!

THE NAME'S THE SAME

The Chinese word 牛 can also mean cow, bull, and even water buffalo.

Some days you might feel like a calm cow. And other days you're full of energy like a bull. Or you might work hard like a water buffalo, which are used in Asia to plow fields.

SIGNS AND SYMBOLS

The Ox is a symbol of good luck and a healthy harvest in China. You'll see images of oxen displayed at Lunar New Year celebrations to bring good luck for the coming year.

REAL OXEN CHEW GRASS AND HAY. But you might prefer noodles or rice much mooo-re!

ELEMENT-ARY

People born in 2021 are Metal Oxen.

But they're no quiet statues. They often are great at smoothing things over and calming people down. Oxen help to keep their pals from fighting.

DREAM JOBS

Because you're not easily rattled, you could be a natural as a surgeon or a vet. Oxen are great in an emergency!

FINDING FRIENDS

Looking for someone who can brighten your day when you're feeling down? It could be your Rat buddy to the rescue! You like hanging out with Snake, too. You're both usually patient.

FEELING LUCKY?

LUCKY NUMBER

1

LUCKY COLOR

GREEN

LUCKY FLOWER

TULIP

NOT SURE IF YOU'RE AN OX?

If you're always honest but some days you're more easygoing than hardworking Ox, go to page 44.

Or go to page 14 to replay the game.

虎

HU

THE TIGER

1926 1938 1950 1962 1974

1986 1998 2010 2022 2034 2046

YOU ARE THE

TIGER

THE TIGER ROARS IN AS THE "KING OF ALL BEASTS" IN CHINA!

You could be brave, full of energy, and adventurous. But be careful not to rush into things! You might make mistakes if you're in too much of a hurry.

You're sometimes tough, but your playful and sweet side makes you fun to be around. You're not afraid to laugh at yourself. Always ready to do what is right, Tigers will leap in and help people who need defending. Your independence and confidence inspire others.

ELEMENT-ARY

If you were born in 2022, you are a Water Tiger.

A Water Tiger is often good at noticing things. What hidden treasures will you find?

DREAM JOBS

Tiger, you were born to be in charge.

You might become the head of a company, a star actor, or a lead singer. Or maybe being outdoors is more your thing? Travel-loving Tigers are eager explorers.

FAMOUSLY

It's no wonder that Olympic gold medalist sprinter Usain Bolt is a Tiger. Tigers are often super speedy and enjoy being the center of attention.

NO ONE WOULD EVER CALL YOU A SOURPUSS...
... but your favorite flavor is sour. You'd probably pick lemonade over orange juice.

JUST FOR FUN

You don't like to sit around and be bored. So traveling is your favorite thing to do—meeting new people, seeing new sights!

FINDING FRIENDS

Feel like doing something active? Invite your Horse or Dog friends over—they're bursting with energy, just like you. You could shoot hoops for hours on end.

But if you want to relax quietly with a pal, calm Pigs are a good pick.

FEELING LUCKY?

LUCKY NUMBERS

7 1 3

LUCKY COLORS

BLUE, PURPLE, GRAY

LUCKY FLOWER

CHRYSANTHEMUM

DON'T FEEL QUITE LIKE A TIGER?
Do you have a killer sense of humor along with being confident? Go to page 52!

Or turn to page 14 to replay the game.

兔

TU

THE RABBIT

1927 1939 1951 1963 1975

1987 1999 2011 2023 2035 2047

YOU ARE THE RABBIT

"HARE"-RAISING ACTIVITIES ARE PROBABLY NOT FOR YOU....

You're usually quiet and gentle, just like a real rabbit. And you tend to be polite and patient, too. Teachers probably wish more students were like you! You might be a little bit too shy sometimes and want to burrow into your own comfortable space. But that doesn't mean you don't like people. You get along with just about every-bunny.

Although you're mostly quiet, you tend to know what you want and you're not afraid to go for it. And every so often, you might even try to show off... but in your polite way, of course.

SIGNS AND SYMBOLS

In Chinese culture, the Rabbit is a symbol of peace. It also represents the moon.

What do you see when you look up at the moon? Some people see a face. In China, people see a rabbit! Legend says that a rabbit lives in a palace on the moon as a reward for being kind to the Jade Emperor.

THE NAME'S THE SAME

The Chinese word 兔 can mean rabbit or hare.

Whether you stay still like a rabbit or leap and prance like a hare, you are a 兔 through and through.

FAMOUSLY

Famous scientist Albert Einstein was a Rabbit. Like many Rabbits, he was quiet and polite, with a gentle sense of humor.

DREAM JOBS

Rabbits are often graceful and musical.

Even shy Rabbits can put aside stage fright and take the spotlight as beautiful dancers or soulful singers.

FINDING FRIENDS

Even though you get along well with everyone, you may like Dog and Goat best.

Dogs are loyal and protective, and Goats are oh so caring. They both warm your furry little heart.

ELEMENT-ARY

2023 is the Year of the Water Rabbit.

People born in this year are extra friendly and easygoing. If their friends keep changing plans at the last minute, no sweat! They'll roll with it.

FEELING LUCKY?

LUCKY NUMBER

4

LUCKY COLOR

GREEN

LUCKY FLOWER

JASMINE

NOT SURE IF YOU'RE A RABBIT?

Are you more serious than patient Rabbit? Go to page 20.

Or turn to page 14 to replay the game.

龍
LONG

THE
DRAGON

1928 1940 1952 1964 1976

1988 2000 2012 2024 2036 2048

YOU ARE THE

DRAGON

DO YOU SOMETIMES FEEL LIKE ROYALTY?

The Chinese once believed that emperors were dragons in a past life! Because of this, the Dragon is viewed as a special sign. In the old days, people thought Dragons were destined for greatness.

Besides being strong, brave, and clever, Dragons are often chatty. You can be very good at talking people into seeing things your way. Just be careful not to talk over your friends. Luckily, you're usually so helpful and generous that people don't mind if you get overexcited.

SAY WHAT?

The common saying 畫龍點睛 (hua long dian jing) translates to "paint a dragon, dot the eyes."

It means adding a final touch to make something perfect... just like everyone thinks Dragons are!

ELEMENT-ARY

If 2024 is your birth year, you are a Wood Dragon.

Your sense of humor might be legendary. Change the world? You're on it, with one unique idea after another!

FINDING FRIENDS

You might get along best with clever Rats and spunky Monkeys. They're happy to follow your big ideas because you lead them on the best adventures.

LEGEND HAS IT

Dragon is the only zodiac sign that isn't a real animal.

In myths from Europe, dragons are scary. They're mean creatures that eat people and steal gold! But Chinese dragons are different. They are bighearted and bring good luck. To the Chinese, they represent power, honor, luck, and success.

FAMOUSLY

Martin Luther King Jr. was everything a Dragon should be. He used his braveness and great mind to bring people together to fight for civil rights.

DREAM JOBS

With your strong, confident personality, you could be pretty much anything you want to be! How about a levelheaded lawyer or an unruffled actor? Or a doctor, since you're often able to make smart, quick decisions.

FEELING LUCKY?

LUCKY NUMBER

2

LUCKY COLOR

SILVER, GOLD

LUCKY GEMSTONE

AMETHYST

DON'T FEEL QUITE LIKE A DRAGON?

You sure are adventurous. But what if you're craving sweet foods, too? Go to page 48.

Or go to page 14 to replay the game.

蛇

SHE

THE

SNAKE

1929 1941 1953 1965 1977

1989 2001 2013 2025 2037 2049

YOU ARE THE

SNAKE

CALM AND COOL SNAKE SLIPS SMOOTHLY INTO SIXTH PLACE IN THE GREAT RACE ...

... not too early, not too late. After all, Snakes are known for their tip-top sense of timing.

Charming and a snappy dresser, you're always ready for action. If you usually finish homework early, it's because Snakes are often organized and like to plan ahead. You might enjoy doing homework because you love to learn!

Sometimes you're sssssssuspiciousssss and have trouble trusting someone new. That's probably why you enjoy being alone or just with a few close friends. But once you get to know a person, you are a very thoughtful friend.

LEGEND HAS IT

In Chinese legend, Nu Wa was the godlike being with the head of a woman and the body of a snake! The stories say that Nu Wa created all humans.

SNAKES USUALLY LIKE BITTER FLAVORS.

Do all your friends want milk chocolate, but you ask for dark? It could be because you're a Snake!

SAY WHAT?

畫蛇添足 (hua she tian zu) is an old saying in Chinese.

It translates to “adding legs to a drawing of a snake.” People use it to mean that you can ruin something by overdoing it. But, Snake, you’re perfect just as you are!

ELEMENT-ARY

2025 is the Year of the Wood Snake.

If you’re a Wood Snake, you might be particularly good at talking to people and understanding how they feel.

FINDING FRIENDS

You often get along great with Rooster.

Maybe it’s because you both dress well. Patient Ox can also be your constant companion. The three of you make a snazzy crew!

DREAM JOBS

Do your friends often ask you for advice?

Besides being wise and patient, you really *get* people. So you would make a helpful teacher or caring counselor.

FEELING LUCKY?

LUCKY NUMBERS

2 8

LUCKY COLORS

RED, BLACK

LUCKY GEMSTONE

OPAL

NOT SURE IF YOU'RE A SNAKE?
Are you a good problem solver but not quite as showy as snazzy Snake? Go to page 60.

Or turn to page 14 to replay the game.

馬

MA

THE HORSE

1930 1942 1954 1966 1978

1990 2002 2014 2026 2038 2050

YOU ARE THE

HORSE

THE GRACEFUL HORSE RACES IN WITH STYLE AND EXCITEMENT!

Like a perfect sports teammate, you tend to be warmhearted and full of energy. Oftentimes you want to be around other people, as real horses do with their herds. You might love being the center of attention. With your cheerful confidence, you usually do have all eyes on you.

But hold your horses! You could be so bouncy and speedy, people might have trouble keeping up with you as you gallop by. Slow down a bit for your friends.

SIGNS AND SYMBOLS

In Chinese culture, horses symbolize good health and success because of their super strength and powerful bodies. Does this sound like you or your Horse friends?

THE SCIENCE

Real horses can sleep standing up, but you would not want to try that! Humans are not built for balance while sleeping. Best to keep lying down in your nice, comfy bed for a restful night.

ELEMENT-ARY

People born in 2026 are Fire Horses.

They're always on the go. When they can't sit still and want to race around, it's because they're all "fired" up!

FINDING FRIENDS

Tiger and Dog both match your high energy. You three could be besties—always ready for action or just fun and games.

JUST FOR FUN

You love being in large crowds.

So you enjoy going to concerts, theaters, or sports events… the more people, the merrier.

DREAM JOBS

If you enjoy all kinds of sports, you could be a great athlete. You could also run your own business with your enthusiasm and confidence.

FEELING LUCKY?

LUCKY NUMBERS

2 7

LUCKY COLORS

SKY BLUE, GREEN, YELLOW

LUCKY FLOWER

ROSE

DON'T FEEL QUITE LIKE A HORSE?

Are you an athlete who doesn't like to bend the rules? Go to page 56.

Or turn to page 14 to replay the game.

羊

YANG

THE GOAT

1931 1943 1955 1967 1979

1991 2003 2015 2027 2039 2051

YOU ARE THE GOAT

EASYGOING GOAT DOESN'T BUTT HEADS WITH FAMILY OR FRIENDS!

Usually caring and kindhearted, you get along with everyone and enjoy being in groups.

You can seem very calm and quiet. But people better watch out! Inner strength helps you stand up for yourself. Go, Goat!

Sometimes you worry too much. When you see your friends feel hurt or sad, you can feel it deeply, too. Thinking of ways to cheer them up could help you get out of feeling down, too. Your imagination could be your superpower!

DREAM JOBS

Being creative, you might want to be an illustrator or a florist, making beautiful flower arrangements. Sure-footed Goats could also be amazing at jobs that involve rock-climbing.

THE SCIENCE

Real goats have rectangular pupils in their eyes. This lets them see out of the corners of their eyes. If you had that skill, your friends would have a much harder time sneaking up on you!

YOU HAVE A REAL SWEET TOOTH.
Given a choice, you will likely pick dessert over anything else. Pass the cupcakes, please!

THE NAME'S THE SAME

Have you heard people talk about the Year of the Sheep, or even the Ram?

That's because the Chinese word 羊 can mean sheep, goat, ram (a male sheep), or ewe (a female sheep)! Sometimes you might be as calm as a sheep or ewe. Other times you could be all fired up like a goat or ram.

FINDING FRIENDS

Because you're both quiet and chill, your idea of a good time with pal Rabbit might be just sitting and enjoying nature together. Playing games with Pig could also be fun—you are both easygoing and honest.

ELEMENT-ARY

If you were born in 2015, you are a maaaah-velous Wood Goat!

You probably have a sharp mind and notice details others don't spot. Your family might ask you to help them find things they've lost.

FEELING LUCKY?

LUCKY NUMBER

7

LUCKY COLOR

RED

LUCKY FLOWER

CARNATION

NOT SURE IF YOU'RE A GOAT?
If your creativity can't be b(l)eat, but you're also extra organized, go to page 16!

Or turn to page 14 to replay the game.

猴

HOU

THE MONKEY

1932 1944 1956 1968 1980

1992 2004 2016 2028 2040 2052

YOU ARE THE

MONKEY

FUN-LOVING AND CHEERFUL MONKEY SWINGS IN, FULL OF ENERGY.

Do you find it hard to sit still sometimes? While Monkeys often are brainy, your fantastic imagination can make you easily distracted. You want to do all the cool stuff and have all the fun with your friends. Monkeys tend to love being around people.

You might suggest playing games with friends. You're usually up for a challenge, and an excellent memory can make you a pro at solving puzzles.

ELEMENT-ARY

Pants on fire? No, you're just the Fire Monkey if you were born in 2016.

Fire Monkeys can be extra imaginative and brilliant at juggling many things at once—like telling jokes while playing a video game and snacking at the same time!

FINDING FRIENDS

Bought a new game? Call your Rat and Dragon buddies over to play. They're just as clever as you, making for an exciting battle of wits.

LEGEND HAS IT

One of the most famous characters in Chinese legend is the Monkey King. He's a mischievous monkey with superpowers and a nose for trouble. He had many exciting adventures and lived to be hundreds of years old. That's why the monkey is a symbol of long life in China.

RIPE FRUIT? YES, PLEASE.
Nothing sounds more delicious to you than juicy fruits—especially yummy peaches.

DREAM JOBS

Monkeys often like to be noticed, so being a comedian or a clown could suit you well. Being able to solve problems quickly can help Monkeys be ace airplane pilots, too.

THE SCIENCE

Bet you share secrets with your best friends. Real monkeys do, too!

Like people, monkeys live in groups of family, friends… and enemies. Scientists have spotted monkeys telling their friends things in secret and hiding this information from others.

FEELING LUCKY?

LUCKY NUMBERS

7 8

LUCKY COLOR

WHITE, BLUE, GOLD

LUCKY FLOWER

POPPY

DON'T FEEL QUITE LIKE A MONKEY?
If you love to monkey around but are extra athletic in your acrobatics, go to page 40!

Or turn to page 14 to replay the game.

雞

JI

THE ROOSTER

1933 1945 1957 1969 1981

1993 2005 2017 2029 2041 2053

YOU ARE THE

ROOSTER

COCK-A-DOODLE-DOO! MAKE WAY FOR ROOSTER, THE TENTH ANIMAL OF THE ZODIAC.

You sometimes strut around with confidence, knowing you look good. Because you can be hardworking, reliable, and funny, people like you. Not many things ruffle your feathers.

You tend to be focused. Building a diorama for homework can be as enjoyable as making a model airplane for fun.

Like real roosters, you usually show up early and often speak your mind. Just be careful you don't crow too much about yourself!

THE NAME'S THE SAME

The Chinese word 雞 can mean chicken and hen, as well as rooster.

When your caring side comes out, you're more like a hen. Your rooster side appears when you stand up for your friends and family.

FEELING HUNGRY?

As a Rooster, you usually prefer to peck at fruit and nuts over other snacks.

ELEMENT-ARY

Were you born in 2017? If so, you are a Fire Rooster. You probably like to talk really, really fast. Your friends might ask you to slow down so they can understand you!

LEGEND HAS IT

Do you help your friends stay out of trouble? Real roosters will do anything to protect their flock of hens. This is probably why, in Chinese legends, roosters can chase away evil spirits.

FINDING FRIENDS

Snake can charm you into being best pals.

But if you need someone you can ace those special school projects with, better call Ox. Trustworthy Ox enjoys working hard, too.

DREAM JOBS

Money-smart and math-minded, you could be an amazing accountant.

Or you might be an excellent engineer—you love math and projects.

FEELING LUCKY?

LUCKY NUMBER

5

LUCKY COLORS

GOLD, BROWN

LUCKY GEMSTONE

CITRINE

NOT SURE IF YOU'RE A ROOSTER?

Are you always on time but think you might be even wiser than Rooster? Go to page 36.

Or turn to page 14 to replay the game.

狗

GOU

THE

DOG

1934 1946 1958 1970 1982

1994 2006 2018 2030 2042 2054

YOU ARE THE DOG

THE MUCH-LOVED AND BRAVE DOG DOESN'T USUALLY GROWL ABOUT MUCH.

You're normally full of energy, but you'd probably describe yourself as a calm person. You are usually helpful, honest, and loyal. If your friends ever need help, you want to be there for them. This makes you a great team player, too. Just don't forget to also take care of yourself!

Dogs are known to be bright, obedient, and good listeners. Just like a real dog, you're usually playful. But you could be stubborn and like to stick to the rules.

ELEMENT-ARY

Do you find yourself a bit shy and bristly in new places or with new people? If you were born in 2018, you are an Earth Dog, who is often more timid than other Dogs. That's okay, though. You warm right up once you get comfortable.

DREAM JOBS

Dogs really, really like to help people... maybe even more than they like to play! You could be a kind nurse. You might also think about being a judge with your honesty.

JUST FOR FUN

Because you are usually peppy and athletic, team sports or martial arts are so your thing. You might also love to take walks, just like real dogs!

FINDING FRIENDS

You work well in groups, but you would rather spend time with a few close friends than go to a big party.

Quiet Rabbit makes a perfect pal to relax with.

But when you want to run around, energetic Tiger is your best bud.

LEGEND HAS IT

In Chinese stories, Tiangou, the Sky Dog, tries to eat the moon. This causes a lunar eclipse (when a shadow covers the moon). People shouted to scare away Tiangou and save the moon.

FAMOUSLY

Chimp expert Jane Goodall was born in the Year of the Dog. Like many Dogs, she was smart and a patient listener—the perfect skills for watching chimpanzees.

FEELING LUCKY?

LUCKY NUMBER

9

LUCKY COLORS

PURPLE, RED, GREEN

LUCKY FLOWER

ROSE

DON'T FEEL LIKE A DOG?
Have so much energy that you want to lead your friends on adventures? Go to page 24.

Or turn to page 14 to replay the game.

豬

ZHU

THE PIG

1935 1947 1959 1971 1983

1995 2007 2019 2031 2043 2055

YOU ARE THE

PIG

LAST BUT NOT LEAST, PIG IS ONE OF THE MOST POPULAR ZODIAC SIGNS!

Pig, you are usually cheerful and smart. Once in a while you can be impatient or a little bit lazy, but remember to lean into your caring and thoughtful side and you will be fine. Your winning personality helps you fit in well anywhere and everywhere.

You're normally in a great mood, and you love to spread joy to others (sometimes at the top of your voice!). This can make you a lovely person to be around.

ELEMENT-ARY

Were you born in 2019?

Then you are an Earth Pig. You can be hog wild with positivity. You always keep your chin (and snout!) up and look on the bright side of everything.

SIGNS AND SYMBOLS

Pigs are a sign of wealth and honesty in China. No wonder they're so popular!

DREAM JOBS

Pigs are known for their love of beauty, so you might dream of becoming a fashion designer or a makeup artist. Or, because Pigs often enjoy luxury, you could be an art dealer selling beautiful paintings.

DO YOU SNIFF OUT DINNER BEFORE ANYONE ELSE?

Real pigs have one of the best senses of smell in the animal world—better than humans and most dogs!

FINDING FRIENDS

You and Goat hit it off well because you are creative. You might like singing made-up songs together!

But when you just want a calm and quiet playdate, Rabbit is the pal to call.

JUST FOR FUN

You might be a fan of baking or cooking since Pigs appreciate good food. Because Pigs also like to spoil their friends and family, you could share those tasty treats with them.

FEELING LUCKY?

LUCKY NUMBERS

2 5 8

LUCKY COLORS

YELLOW, BROWN

LUCKY FLOWER

HYDRANGEA

NOT SURE IF YOU'RE A PIG?

If you get along with everyone but are quieter than a Pig, go to page 28.

Or turn to page 14 to replay the game.

EVEN MORE

ANIMALS

STILL NOT SURE YOU'VE FOUND YOUR PERFECT ZODIAC ANIMAL?

The twelve animals in this book are the traditional ones for the Chinese zodiac, but not all countries use these animals in their zodiac. Here are some of their cool substitutes that you could be more like.

VIETNAM

Cat takes the place of Rabbit in the Vietnamese zodiac. Meow-velous! Cats are supposed to be calm and artistic, and are also thought to be strong and powerful.

Outside of Vietnam, the Cat appears in other versions of the Great Race story, too. Some say that Rat and Cat were both riding on Ox's back. Rat pushed Cat into the water, causing Cat to arrive in the thirteenth spot. Because only the first twelve animals could be in the Chinese zodiac, Cat missed being included. In another version, Rat forgot to wake Cat up before the race, so Cat couldn't take part.

Either way, the result is that Cat never forgave Rat. That's why the two are enemies to this day!

THAILAND

In Thailand, Dragon is replaced by the Naga, a magical serpent. People born in the Naga year are said to be brainy, kindhearted, and travel-loving.

Some Thai people also replace Pig with Elephant! Elephants are rare in China, but they are an important animal in Thailand.

JAPAN

Japan celebrates the Year of the Boar instead of the Year of the Pig. Boar is anything but boar-ing though! They are known for being strong and brave, willing to tackle anything that comes their way.

UNIQUELY YOU

SO, DID YOU MEET YOUR MATCH?

You might have qualities that are similar to your zodiac birth sign. Or you might have found that your birth sign doesn't match your unique personality—perhaps you identify with a completely different animal! You might even have found that you identify with lots of animals at the same time. For example, you could have the adventurous spirit of a Dragon, the mischievous nature of a Monkey, but also enjoy your quiet, personal space like a Rabbit. You would be a Dragon-Monkey-Rabbit!

Each of us is a lovely tangle of traits, and no single label can describe us completely.

Share this book with your friends and family. Have them look up their signs by birth years and see how well the animals describe them. Be sure to play the game on page 14 with them, too! You could all find out something new about each other.

While the zodiac is a super-fun way to learn about yourself and your friends, it doesn't mean you need to live by it. If you were born a Rabbit but want to be an engineer like a Rooster, go for it!

REMEMBER, YOU ARE UNIQUE.
YOU CAN BE *ANYTHING* YOU WANT TO BE!

AUTHOR'S NOTE

I was born in the Year of the Dragon. Like a Dragon, I'm generous and enjoy helping people. But I'm afraid I am not adventurous like a Dragon should be. I like to burrow in my comfy chair like a Rabbit, and sometimes I'm easily distracted like a Monkey.

As a child living in Hong Kong, I excitedly celebrated everything about the Lunar New Year—from special foods to getting red money envelopes.

My father taught me about the Chinese zodiac when I was little. My sister and I had a blast comparing and teasing each other about our personalities. I wanted to write this book so that you could have as much fun with this ancient practice as my sister and I did!

ILLUSTRATOR'S NOTE

I am definitely a very chatty Dragon, though I don't always feel very brave. The warm hearted nature of Horses is something aspirational, but maybe it's because I liked drawing horses as a kid. . . .

I grew up in a vibrant Chinese community in Los Angeles and remember feeling very excited when my zodiac year would come around (a Dragon's trait perhaps?). My parents said it was the "Ben Ming Nian," which roughly translates to your birth sign year, when growth and change are extra turbulent.

In Chinese culture, red is traditionally seen as a boost of luck, so make sure you have some nearby during your zodiac year to help guide you! (My lucky charm of choice is a jade doughnut necklace on a red thread.)

Phaidon Press Limited
2 Cooperage Yard
London E15 2QR

Phaidon Press Inc.
111 Broadway
New York, NY 10006

Phaidon SARL
55, rue Traversière
75012 Paris

phaidon.com

First published 2026

Artwork created digitally and painted with gouache on paper.

Fact check and authenticity read by Zijia Zhuang

ISBN 978 1 83729 213 4 (US edition)
007-0826

A CIP catalog record for this book is available from the Library of Congress.

Printed in China

Commissioning Editor: Netta Rabin (Snake)
Project Editors: Rachel Craig-McFeely (Tiger) and Maya Gartner (Goat)
Production Controller: Rebecca Price (Dragon)
Design: Meagan Bennett (Rat-Pig)